Nature's Balady

Shivani Mehrotra

BookLeaf Publishing

India | USA | UK

Made with ❤ on the BookLeaf Publishing Platform
www.bookleafpub.in
www.bookleafpub.com

Dedication

To the mountains, where silence finds words,
To the black forest, where tranquility resides
To the ocean, where I want to sit by and listen to the waves

Preface

This collection of poems depicts random thoughts and feelings that emerged from moments filled with serenity in life. It is in those quiet moments that creativity struck and music of silence could be heard and observed. Each verse is a feeling felt within or a thought imagined that celebrates closeness with nature and was selectively tended to. Each poem carries its own character that is distinctly identified from others-representing the uniqueness of each imagined thought and a bubble carrying feelings.

As I wrote these poems I found myself returning to the idea of simplicity of nature, appreciating its stillness and the consequent creativity that emerges as one surrenders to its beauty and magic. These poems are written with the intention of giving happiness to the readers, taking them into the depths of within through an imaginative power of words. It is my hope that these poems will soothe the readers through the kaleidoscope of changing seasons of nature.

Acknowledgements

This book has been possible because of my parents, my constant cheerleaders. Their continuous guidance and support has pushed me to finally come out with this collection of poems and let my readers know the 'words' that await them. To the reader—thank you for taking out the time to dive into these words.

1. Rains & Rivers

Parched o my soul
Blooming daisies wait for
Those pearl drops
& the rivers & the
Rhythms seem to slow.
Wish if you were here
That lovely soul
Where the girl in me waits to glow
Shine like daffodils and those curly drops.
Nothing is there
I seem to be lost
Holding onto hope,
Waiting for the arrival of
That after rain rainbow.

2. O Rain

O rain!
I know you were not needed this time
Or maybe you were
But o rain
The night is gonna be a melody
To the tune of vintage melodies
Or jazz
Or maybe bohemian
The night is gonna be pleasant
With soothing aroma
Of sandy
And potpourri
To quench the summer heat
O dear rain
You were needed.

3. The Swiss Rain

Alps, snow clad mountains
Mysterious and bold
The nightime and windchimes
In the backdrop.
Cloudy skies and starry star of Harder Kulm
It rained o so heavy
The streets are empty,
As I see the view from my window
The glistening streetlight on the wet roads
This grandeur of mighty mountains not roars
But stand in silence still
They call for beauty and depths
For the next morning it snowed
And decorated the view of blues in whites.

4. September Rains

Raining like thunderstorm
No, its not the monsoon
Its raining autumn
Mellow it seems
But somewhere or underneath
Its brewing
Cinnamon rolls, potpourri and coffee beans.
The sun is not so sunny anymore
It's earthy, simple and green algae
The rainy sound, the cool air
Whirls and swirls with the raindrops
For the September rains are carefree.

5. Last Months of Summer

5

With leaves turning gold
Retreating monsoon
The clouds
The rains,
Gave a beautiful ending to summer.
Festooning the soiree
The blooms turned yellow, green, red and gold
Laying the red carpet for
Winter to unfold
Lit up the fireplace
And let the songs turn to cocoon.

6. The Red Autumn

Maple leaves,
Pine leaves,
Bougainvillea leaves,
Or just leaves
Sway in air
And fall on the ground
To the rhythm of October air,
It is the season of royalty
As the leaves turn golden with a pinch of red, purple too
Seems as if they
Indicate the setting of sun in the
Northern hemisphere.
Maybe it is the void
That needs to be accepted,
Of winters,
That will long, how long
Before the spring brings its blooming solitaire.

7. Winters

The snow covered mountains
The white skies, not blue
O the winters
The stillness, the silence
I bow down to you.
Falling snow like raindrops
The Balsam firs are snow clad
All around a 'White Mirage'
Not a ray of sun
Yet there is light
A sheen of white
Whispering that it's day time.
Slowly the night arrives
And the fireplace lits up
The sky turns blue
And I hear the sparks of burning wood
O the winters
O the winters.

8. Snowflakes

The white crystal droplets
turned into flakes
like shredded ice
like saw dust
like pieces of paper
the frozen flakes swirl and float on earth with breezy
chilly air.

They swirl, they dance
the white crystal shreds
Hexagonal
Each distinct and has its own sweet rhythm

The water drops,
the mist,
the fog frozen into these snowflakes,
as if the sun is expressing its rays through these white
snowflakes

The white snowflakes animate the golden sunrays
with golden strokes on its surface
they are platinum pristine and finely encapsulate the
white sun, through floral or pine design
Uniquely crafted,

revealing the beauty of eternity in those fleeting moments.

9. Sunshine on my Balcony

Here after the stillness of winters
Finally!
I have got my sunrays of spring on my balcony.
After months of irrevocable winters stillness
I found the golden rays of sunshine.
They are here to stay for as long as I can think.
The morning chirruping of birds
& music of spring surrounding serendipity, I got my rays
of spring.
It sounds like melody and golden rays of sun
I welcome them and topsy-turvy as I get ready for
season to bloom.
I pen some initial thoughts
As I welcome the first rays of Sun
On my balcony.

10. Sunrise

I see a northern star
Shining above
Dawn it is
Billow
Like the sea surf
Far below it is the shades of pink, orange and yellow
Blue defining the backdrop
Citylights dimming
The day slowly rising
As if, after a long night
The green avenue of trees waiting to adorn this day
And the chirruping of the birds like a soft dainty musical
rhythm.

11. Chasing the Moon

Shining from the chinks of the cloudy sky
The dark night sky
I wonder looking at the moon.
As the city lights pass by
And the whooshing train
Takes me home
I ponder looking at the moon.
A silent admiration
Of the beauty that blooms
O the moon
Nearing full moon
A gibbous moon.

12. Lavender Fields

Shades of hue
Purple dew
Pink, purple, rosy, wine, berry, cherry, orangish shine
Fields of lavender & shades of green
Adorn the beauty under the open skies
Golden hour, sitting in white
On the grass
Airplane and birds adorn the skies
Lying carefree in lavender fields.
The heart is young and smiles shine
Dancing solemnly in awe of pink florals, lavender fields.
The air is calm, silence is balmy, spring inside-out,
adorning the beauty of lavender fields.

13. Pearl Drops on Rose Petal

Dew drops on the rose petal
Big small and mini,
The rose petal looks o so dainty.
I fancy the dew drops
On the roses
In a garden
Mesmerizing it is
Or is it the nature's ecstasy!

14. A Silent Ode

Merrymaking greens of Lauterbrunnen
Grindelwald
The mountains and the sunny warmth
The road that takes me home
A place where my heart lays
& stays.
The blue ribbon and white air
Aroma of cheese and cup of coffee
Streets of Interlaken
Surrounded in silence
And
Calmness of the valley.
That silly jovial girl
Adorned with flowers and curls
Dances under the stars on the grass
In the lap of Switzerland.

15. Leaving Valley

I see a sea of green through my eyes,
Mellow is the breeze that brushes my hair,
Yellow are the daffodils ,
and the doves are white.
As I drive my bike,
Passing by are the blue skies.
Herd of sheep rearing in the grass,
Freezing air,
O so fair
Are the valleys
As I can see in my rear.
The blooms are blooming,
Such bounty of nature,
Splendid suns and the moons,
Star gazing has become so rare.
Such is the city life,
O my silly,
Why did I leave my pretty valley.

16. The Norway Sun

17

The Norway Sun
Oh the land of midnight sun!
Where the day never dies and
The night never comes alive
Yet it is the cold warmth
That keeps alive!
I bow down to this beauty
Where Sun & Moon
The crescent bliss
Sunny beams
Stay together
A
Safe haven.

17. Barcelona Nights

The yellow lights
In the Barcelona nights
Pint of tequila
And o-so shots!
The wilderness inside
Goes high
The night air
Touches the hair
And those kindle
Joys and laughs
Amidst the whirls of like
Backstreet boys.
This madness of young nights.

18. Morning Glitz

Manicured nails
Smoothened hair
Crispy white shirt
With a blue jeans pair
What's new
In the air?
Pretty pink peck smile
And glitter in eyes
A golden chain
Around the neck
And diamonds in ears
What seems new
In the air?
Juicy aromas
Champagnes
And dainty perfumes
Dollops of ice cream
In the exquisite cafes
And sunny summer delight
Adorn the view
Somethings are new!

19. The Orange Bliss

Orange they would say
The tangy ones they would say
The vibrant ones they would say
Alive are the oranges
With a tinge of happiness in it
To turn the whites of winters
Into sunny vibes.

20. Cherishing In-Out

I am fed up
Fed up of some things.
Some things that are
Useless and worth dumping.
Dumping the undue stress & thoughts
That have built an unnecessary mountain.
Mountains of lush green, & flowers
are worth climbing.
Climbing the thorns & weeds
As I move ahead in journey.
Journey towards creating the fresh new me.
Me wishing to re-ignite the spark of joy in me.
The spark of joy that nurtures me
Nurture myself
So that I can cherish what in-out I have in me.

21. Dear Mom

The world was beautiful
When I was in your lap
And we were in the zoo,
Only the monkeys
The tigers
The racoons
The bears
Were caged
And we were not.
The world was beautiful
When the sun rays kissed us
With the winter warmth
The smile and laughs were real
With glee and joy
Unlike the put up smiley face
That I have to carry amidst the storms
Those giggles and chuckles
Were not only confined to lips but reflected through eyes
and heart.
In a world full of disdain
You seem to be a ray of hope
That first and last sliver of warmth and cozy heart.

www.ingramcontent.com/pod-product-compliance
Lightning Source LLC
Chambersburg PA
CBHW061325140726

47998CB00007B/2558